▶ YouTubers

JOJO SIWA

JESSICA RUSICK

**Checkerboard
Library**

An Imprint of Abdo Publishing
abdobooks.com

abdobooks.com

Published by Abdo Publishing, a division of ABDO, PO Box 398166, Minneapolis, Minnesota 55439. Copyright © 2020 by Abdo Consulting Group, Inc. International copyrights reserved in all countries. No part of this book may be reproduced in any form without written permission from the publisher. Checkerboard Library™ is a trademark and logo of Abdo Publishing.

Printed in the United States of America, North Mankato, Minnesota
102019
012020

THIS BOOK CONTAINS RECYCLED MATERIALS

Design: Sarah DeYoung, Mighty Media, Inc.
Production: Mighty Media, Inc.
Editor: Rebecca Felix
Cover Photograph: Shutterstock Images
Interior Photographs: Bruce Glikas/Getty Images, p. 7; Dave Nelson/N&S SYNDICATION/AP Images, p. 25; Frazer Harrison/Getty Images, p. 9; Jerritt Clark/Getty Images, p. 15; John Salangsang/Invision/AP Images, p. 13; Jordan Strauss/Invision/AP Images, p. 5; Mighty Media, Inc., pp. 17, 19, 20, 21 ("Boomerang" sticker), 29 (bottom); Shutterstock Images, p. 21 (JoJo with hair bows, JoJo sign, JoJo merchandise on shelves); Sthanlee Mirador/Sipa USA/AP Images, pp. 11, 27, 28, 29 (top, bottom); Tess_Trunk/iStockphoto, pp. 6, 20, 21, 24, 28; Wesley Hitt/Getty Images, p. 23

Library of Congress Control Number: 2019943370

Publisher's Cataloging-in-Publication Data
Names: Rusick, Jessica, author.
Title: JoJo Siwa / by Jessica Rusick
Description: Minneapolis, Minnesota : Abdo Publishing, 2020 | Series: YouTubers | Includes online resources and index.
Identifiers: ISBN 9781532191831 (lib. bdg.) | ISBN 9781644943618 (pbk.) | ISBN 9781532178566 (ebook)
Subjects: LCSH: Siwa, JoJo, 2003- (Joelle Joanie Siwa)--Juvenile literature. | YouTube (Firm)--Juvenile literature. | Internet celebrities--Biography--Juvenile literature. | Singers--Biography--Juvenile literature. | Dancers--Biography--Juvenile literature. | Internet videos--Juvenile literature. | Dance moms (Television program)--Juvenile literature. | Nickelodeon (Television network)--Juvenile literature.
Classification: DDC 646.7092--dc23

Contents

Get to Know JoJo

JoJo Siwa is a YouTuber, dancer, singer, actress, and social media **influencer**. She is known for her YouTube channels Its JoJo Siwa and JoJo Siwa TV. There, JoJo posts **vlogs**, music videos, and more. JoJo's fun content, energetic personality, and glittering fashion sense have made her a star.

JoJo was first in the spotlight on dance-themed reality TV shows. But it was her YouTube videos that brought her great fame. Over just a few years of sharing content, JoJo has earned millions of fans and built an empire around her personality. In addition to YouTube channels, there are JoJo songs, clothing, accessories, games, books, and more!

No matter the product or platform, JoJo uses her fame to **promote** kindness and **positivity**. She also promotes anti-bullying and encourages having fun. Fans around the world are inspired by her messages and style. From a very young age, JoJo captured people's attention.

JoJo has won several awards. These include Nickelodeon Kids' Choice Awards for Favorite Viral Music Artist in 2017 and Favorite Musical YouTube Creator in 2018.

Little Girl, Big Dreams

Joelle Joanie "JoJo" Siwa was born on May 19, 2003, in Omaha, Nebraska. Her parents are Tom and Jessalynn. Tom is a **chiropractor**. Jessalynn teaches dance. JoJo has one older brother, Jayden.

From a young age, JoJo loved to dance. Her mom's dance studio was like a second home. There, JoJo watched older girls prepare for dance competitions. She dreamed of being in the spotlight herself. JoJo wanted to be a star and dance on TV one day.

JoJo sometimes helped food vendors at dance competitions she attended. She especially loved to make and eat nachos. Today, JoJo has a nacho maker in her house!

Jessalynn also believed JoJo could be a star. She became JoJo's dance instructor. JoJo performed in her first dance competition in 2005 at age two.

Jayden, Tom, JoJo, and Jessalynn Siwa.
Jayden is three years older than JoJo.
He also has a YouTube channel.

When JoJo was five, she competed in AMTC. It was a talent showcase for young dancers and actors. This showcase allowed talent agencies to discover new talent. Many AMTC performers later became TV stars.

After competing, JoJo went on several **auditions**. She did not get any roles. But these auditions taught JoJo that dance could be more than fun. It could be a career!

Dance Darling

JoJo continued to perform in dance competitions throughout her early childhood. But being on TV never left her mind. When she was eight years old, JoJo **auditioned** for the TV show *Abby's Ultimate Dance Competition*.

On this show, young dancers competed to win $100,000 and a **scholarship** to the Joffrey Ballet School in New York. They were coached and judged by dance instructor Abby Lee Miller. JoJo was already a huge fan of the show, and of Miller.

After a few rounds of auditioning, JoJo made the show! She starred on the second season in September 2013. At nine years old, JoJo was the season's youngest dancer. This sometimes made it difficult for her to compete with more experienced dancers. But JoJo's energy and outgoing personality stood out during performances.

JoJo placed fifth on *Abby's Ultimate Dance Competition*. It became the first of many shows she starred on. In 2014, JoJo joined the cast of *Dance Moms*.

JoJo and *Dance Moms* castmates attend a Nickelodeon event in 2015.

Dance Moms featured a group of dancers also coached by Miller. Each week on the show, JoJo and her castmates learned a group dance. Some dancers also learned solo or duo dances. Then, dancers would perform at competitions.

Unlike on *Abby's Ultimate Dance Competition*, dancers on *Dance Moms* were not **eliminated** each week. So, JoJo starred on the show until its sixth season in 2016.

JoJo's schedule was very busy during her time on *Dance Moms*. Often, her days started at 8 a.m. with homeschooling. An advanced student, JoJo had been homeschooled for all of her schooling except kindergarten. Homeschooling allowed her to move at a faster pace than in a traditional classroom setting.

After two or three hours of homeschooling, JoJo took a break for lunch. Then, her work on *Dance Moms* began.

The show filmed from 12 p.m. to 4 p.m. Tuesday through Saturday. But JoJo's dance routine didn't always end when filming did! Some days, she continued to practice dance until bedtime at 10:30 p.m.

Despite the long hours, dance remained fun for JoJo. She liked working with her coach and fellow dancers. JoJo also had a good reception from viewers. *Dance Moms* fans liked her upbeat attitude and bright, colorful style. JoJo had become a TV star! But her fame was rising on another platform too.

JoJo became friends with several *Dance Moms* castmates, including Maddie Ziegler. The show also made Maddie a star.

Parallel Pursuit

Dance and TV stardom weren't JoJo's only childhood pursuits. In 2015, while competing on *Dance Moms*, she also launched her own YouTube channel.

JoJo named her channel It's JoJo Siwa. Dancing star Autumn Miller was the channel's inspiration. JoJo loved Miller's YouTube videos, which focused on life as a dancer.

But JoJo didn't begin by posting about dance. Her first YouTube video showed fans how to make a bracelet out of duct tape. Then, JoJo posted dance stretch tutorials. Soon, she began posting **vlogs**.

JoJo's vlogs revealed her everyday life. In her first one, JoJo filmed herself and her mother at the airport before a flight. In another, JoJo gave fans a tour of her bedroom.

JoJo also answered fan questions on a weekly installment called JoJo's Juice. At the end of each JoJo's Juice video, JoJo dumped juice on her head! This showed viewers her silly sense of humor.

JoJo holds Jiffpom at a 2015 event. Jiffpom is a fellow social media star! He became famous on Instagram.

The same fun, goofy energy that made JoJo a TV star made her a success online. Her popularity on YouTube grew.

13

Study, Schedule & Style

JoJo became interested in all things YouTube. She studied videos by famous YouTubers and was inspired to improve her own videos. JoJo asked her mom to make computer class part of JoJo's homeschool classes.

Jessalynn agreed. So, in addition to regular schoolwork, JoJo spent hours researching video editing software and methods. What she learned helped improve her videos.

JoJo also learned directly from YouTubers like Colleen Ballinger. Ballinger has a popular channel called Miranda Sings, where she posts as a character of the same name. JoJo met Ballinger, who shared some advice.

Ballinger told JoJo that successful YouTubers post videos often, and on a schedule. This way, viewers know when to expect new content. So, JoJo worked to post **consistently**, earning more and more fans. By 2016, JoJo was gaining hundreds of thousands of **subscribers** each month!

JoJo's personality and style also earned her fans. JoJo showed off her fashion sense in her videos. She wore bright colors, large hair bows, and sparkles. Fans loved JoJo's bright outlook and clothing. But sometimes, JoJo also faced online **negativity**.

Fellow YouTuber Colleen Ballinger wears a shirt supporting JoJo's fashion staple of large hair bows.

"Boomerang" & Bullying

JoJo had many fans online. But not every viewer praised her videos. Some posted mean comments about her. JoJo called these people haters.

Haters had bullied JoJo since she first appeared on TV. They made fun of her appearance, personality, and dance skills.

This **negativity** hurt JoJo's feelings. She knew she couldn't make haters go away. But she also felt she could use her YouTube channel to make the world a nicer place.

JoJo knew many kids faced bullying online and in person. She wanted to spread an anti-bullying message. And she decided to use music to do it.

In May 2016, JoJo **debuted** the music video "Boomerang" on her YouTube channel. Songwriters helped her use the song to communicate a message. When you throw a boomerang, it comes back. JoJo thought this was a great way for fans to picture bouncing back from bullying!

BOOMERANG

JoJo's popular song "Boomerang" includes the lyrics, "Won't let the haters get their way."

"Boomerang" was a success! The music video received 16 million views in its first two weeks. Its popularity grew as JoJo's fame rose.

One year after "Boomerang" **debuted**, it had received more than 200 million views. By 2019, it was JoJo's most-watched video with more than 700 million views.

JoJo also used other social media channels to **promote** her anti-bullying message. She was active on Twitter and Instagram. In 2016, JoJo created the hashtags #Siwanatorz and #PeaceOutHaterz for use on these platforms.

Siwanatorz are what JoJo calls her fans. To her, Siwanatorz are strong people who spread kindness. They say "peace out" to haters!

JoJo encouraged her fans to show off their Siwanator pride using the hashtags. In one 2016 post, JoJo asked fans to post pictures of themselves wearing mismatched socks. This was to prove that differences didn't matter.

Since their creation, JoJo's hashtags have been posted by fans tens of thousands of times. Meanwhile, JoJo continued to find new ways to promote **positivity** on- and off-screen.

JoJo's hashtag #PeaceOutHaterz appears on the cover of her first book, published in 2017.

JoJo Bows

"Boomerang" was not JoJo's only project to **debut** in 2016. That same year, she also brought hair bows to fans worldwide.

Since she was very young, JoJo has worn large hair bows. When she starred on *Dance Moms*, these bows became part of her **signature** look.

JoJo said her bows gave her power and **confidence**. That's how she wanted her fans to feel too! JoJo partnered with accessory store Claire's to sell her bows. Claire's debuted them in 100 stores. The bows sold so well that Claire's offered them in more stores. By 2019, JoJo's bows were sold in all 3,500 Claire's stores worldwide.

JoJo's bows are about more than just fashion. They also relate to her anti-bullying movement.

In 2019, JoJo owned more than 1,000 bows.

New Channels

Clothing & Accessories: JoJo sells clothing, bows, and other accessories inspired by her style.

Nickelodeon: In September 2018, Nickelodeon aired *The JoJo and BowBow Show Show* on its YouTube Channel. It was a show about JoJo and her dog, BowBow.

Music: JoJo has released several songs and planned a 2019 concert tour.

More: JoJo-themed products are sold around the world! These include dolls, decor, toys, makeup, and more.

JoJo says wearing one of her bows helps identify the wearer as a Siwanator who believes in ending bullying. She sees her bows as standing for kindness and **positivity**.

Fan Influencer

As JoJo's bows took off, her YouTube success continued to soar. By 2017, she was posting on two channels. JoJo Siwa TV was for **vlogs**. Its JoJo Siwa was for music videos, product announcements, and videos with other YouTube stars.

JoJo planned, shot, and edited all her videos herself. Her mom also helped JoJo create content. She drove JoJo to stores and bought supplies for craft videos. Sometimes, Jessalynn also appeared in videos.

JoJo worked hard to keep a regular posting schedule. She sometimes spent late nights and early mornings filming and editing videos. Her videos let fans into her everyday life. And JoJo's life was anything but boring!

Some Its JoJo Siwa videos featured JoJo doing silly challenges or sharing behind-the-scenes looks at music videos. JoJo also posted videos with fellow famous YouTubers, such as Ballinger. In one, JoJo gave Ballinger's character Miranda Sings a makeover inspired by JoJo's style.

JoJo spent her 14th birthday in 2017 at a Walmart in Arkansas. Fans met her at the superstore for the debut of new JoJo products.

As a YouTube star, JoJo was a social media **influencer**. An influencer has a large, active fan base on social media. Fans connect to influencers because of their **authenticity**. This helps influencers gain larger followings.

The relationship between **influencers** and their fans also helps influencers sell products. In the past, companies often spent millions of dollars to **promote** products in advertisements. But JoJo could use social media to reach millions of fans for free.

In addition to her other content, JoJo posted videos updating her fans about new JoJo products. In 2017, she partnered with superstore Target to launch the clothing line JoJo's Closet.

Target didn't advertise JoJo's Closet at all. Instead, it had JoJo film and post a YouTube video about it! Because fans like and trust JoJo, many of her clothes sold out quickly.

Many of JoJo's other products sell out quickly too. These include JoJo-themed dolls, nail polish, slime, books, and more. To many fans, JoJo feels more like a close friend than a celebrity.

VIP Post

In 2017, JoJo and Ballinger's character Miranda Sings made slime together. The video received more than 45 million views!

JoJo greets fans at live events and concerts. She also takes time to snap photos with fans she meets in her daily life.

Nickelodeon & Next

By 2017, JoJo was a social media star. That year, she also began a new career path. She partnered with children's network Nickelodeon to make TV shows, music, and more.

JoJo's partnership with Nickelodeon led to a change in her dance career too. JoJo no longer danced in competitions. Instead, she danced in her own music videos!

At first, being at Nickelodeon felt unfamiliar to JoJo. But within six months, she felt like part of the network family. JoJo began featuring Nickelodeon in her YouTube posts.

In 2019, JoJo continued to upload new videos almost daily. Its JoJo Siwa had more than 9 million **subscribers**. JoJo Siwa TV had more than 3.5 million subscribers. Altogether, JoJo's videos had more than 2 billion views.

In the future, JoJo hopes to find continued success online, in stores, and with fans. But more than anything, she wants to keep **promoting** values she believes in. As JoJo says, "The only way to live your best life is to be yourself!"

In 2019, JoJo won a Nickelodeon Kids' Choice Award for Favorite Social Music Star.

Timeline

2003

JoJo Siwa is born on May 19 in Omaha, Nebraska.

2008

JoJo participates in the talent competition AMTC.

2014

JoJo stars on *Dance Moms.*

2005

JoJo performs in her first solo dance competition.

2013

JoJo stars on the second season of *Abby's Ultimate Dance Competition* and places fifth.

2015

JoJo begins posting regular videos on YouTube.

2017

JoJo partners with children's network Nickelodeon to release new products and content.

2016

JoJo's song "Boomerang" premieres on YouTube. It will become her most-watched video. JoJo's bows debut in Claire's stores.

2019

JoJo has more than 9 million subscribers and 2 billion views on YouTube.

Glossary

audition—a short performance to test someone's ability. To audition is to give a trial performance showcasing personal talent as a musician, a singer, a dancer, or an actor.

authenticity—showing a realness or being genuine.

chiropractor—a doctor who treats people who are sick or in pain by adjusting body structures.

confidence—faith in oneself and one's powers.

consistently—in a way that continues to develop or happen in the same way.

debut (DAY-byoo)—to first appear or to present or perform something for the first time.

eliminate—to get rid of or remove.

influencer—a social media personality with a large fan base, and who uses his or her popularity to sell products, start trends, or gain more followers.

negativity—related to something that is bad or hurtful.

positivity—related to something that is kind, good, or helpful.

promote—to contribute to the growth, prosperity, or popularity of an item, brand, or person through advertising or support.

scholarship—money or aid given to help a student continue his or her studies.

signature—something that sets apart or identifies an individual, group, or company.

subscriber—someone who signs up to receive something on a regular basis.

vlog—a video log that tells about someone's personal opinions, activities, and experiences.

Online Resources

Booklinks
NONFICTION NETWORK
FREE! ONLINE NONFICTION RESOURCES

To learn more about JoJo Siwa, please visit **abdobooklinks.com** or scan this QR code. These links are routinely monitored and updated to provide the most current information available.

Index